THE POWER SQUAD DETECTIVES

Dream Independent Press

About the Author

Savannah Darish is an imaginative 8-year-old who loves reading, experimenting, and drawing. Writing stories is her favourite way to share her creative world with others. This is her very first book, and she hopes it brings smiles to many faces.

When she's not writing, you'll find her deep in a book or trying out fun experiments at home. Savannah dreams of becoming a scientist one day—and maybe writing more stories along the way!

THE POWER SQUAD DETECTIVES

SAVANNAH DARISH

Dream Independent Press

The Power Squad Detectives | Savannah Darish

Published by DREAM INDEPENDENT PRESS

Dream Independent Press is a part of Dream Bookbindery,

whose addresses can be found at www.dreambookbindery.com

First Published by Dream Independent Press in 2025

ISBN 9789390800971

Typeset in Comic Sans MS by TEAM: MAAYA, Kerala
Cover Design by TEAM: MAAYA

Printed and Bound in India

This book is produced from independently certified FSC® paper to ensure responsible forest management.

INDEX

ROBOT BANDITS

Hi! It's me ***SAVANNAH!*** And I'm one of the ***POWER SQUAD!!!***

So if you are wondering what this adventure is about, let's dive in! So lately we've been traveling around a lot. Last week we went to Ethiopia. This week we are planning to go to Tanzania! On the flight, I was snipping pictures of the breathtaking view while ***Rian*** and ***Isabelle*** were making friends. When we stepped out, we put on our sunscreen, because we heard that Tanzania is a burning hot place.

But what we saw made us leap into action. People were running around and shouting, "Help! It's a robot attack!".

We pulled out our magic flowers, clicked the secret button, and transformed ourselves, and it was time to save the city! I climbed a monkey bar in a nearby park and knocked down 2 of the robots! Then I shot jets of water at both of them. After that, we worked together. **Isabelle** shot clouds at them so they won't be able to see. **Rian** shot webs at them to capture them, I shot water at them so they would power down, and **Gian** trapped them in his tough grass cages.

Then we saw a few robots robbing a bank. We thought that defeating them would be just as easy as defeating the other ones, but nope, I tried to kick one of the robots, but I went flying back! These robots were stronger than we thought.

Hmm... If these robots are stronger than us, then we have to be sneakier than them.

We have to find a way to discover their weakness!

"I know their weakness! I know their weakness!" Isabelle cried.

"What is it?!" I asked.

She said, "A charge remover!"

"Where can we get one?" Rian asked.

"In the hardware shop over there," Isabelle replied.

"Go get one", I said. "We will hold them

back.

So **Isabelle** ran to the shop, snatched a charge remover and screamed to the owner, "I'll pay later!" By the time Isabelle returned, **Rian** and I were flat as pancakes!

"Finally, you're here." I managed to say, though I was out of breath.

She showed the charge remover.

"Yay", I screamed.

Just then, the robots came in stomping.

Opps. I might have been a bit too loud. But that didn't stop us. Oh, did I mention that she took 2 charge removers? Did I? Whatever. Umm... where was I? Oh yes, so **Rian** and **Isabelle** pointed their charge removers at the robots, and their power was dropping. Then I knocked them down. Those were the last robots we needed to defeat.

WOW! A fantastic adventure on our first day here!

"There's just one more thing I need to do", Isabelle said.

She went to the shop where she took

the charge removers and paid 4$ to the owner.

I yawned. "Let's go sleep", I said.

A hero needs good rest, right? The next day, there was a huge and grand ceremony held in our honor! The king even gave us an enormous royal bag full of gold coins! It was so big that not even us three together could lift it! So we had to drag it to the hotel.

PECULIAR PLANTS

Hi! My name is **Savannah**, and I'm one of the **Power SQUAD**. In our last story, we went to Tanzania. Now, today we are going to Somalia! As always, we sat together, and people would go crazy when they would see us and also ask for autographs, lots and lots of autographs.

I don't mean to be snooty, but sometimes people drive us mad! We were tired of signing papers, so we slept, or at least. It was too noisy for any of us to sleep.

"We're trying to sleep!" I shouted, then the crowd around us which was once very noisy, fell silent.

"Ah, that's better," I said and snuggled into my blanket.

Isabelle, **Rian** and **Gian** did so too. When we reached, we realized we were in the town square! Just like on the aeroplane, people had gone crazy! Even a few small children ran to us, well, not a few. Every child came to us! Reporters, adults, kids. So many people surrounded us!

Just then, a blue cloud of smoke arose from some part of the town square, then we could not see! When the smoke cleared, we realized **Isabelle** was missing! Everyone looked at each other and then went wild.

"Savannah!, Rian!, Gian!" a muffled voice shouted.

"Isabelle, is that you?!" Gian shouted.

This time there was no answer, even though we listened intendely.

"I heard her voice from this way!" Rian shouted. "Let's go!"

Then we saw a sight that you won't believe! The garden in the town square had huge carnivorous plants! There were enormous tulips that were alive!

Gian said, "These plants can eat us, but they have to poison us first with their poisonous petals!".

We gasped.

"Poisonous petals!" Rian shouted.

Then the plants turned to face us!

"We need to get out of here!" Rian cried!

"But how!?" I said in alarm.

"Does anyone have any meat?" Gian asked.

"Do you really think it is the right time for a snack?" Rian asked.

"No," Gian said. "But if we throw the meat, the tulips will get distracted and we can go around!"

"That is a double genius idea. Why did I not think of that!" I said.

"Anyways I've got some meat!" I pulled it out, threw it to my left and we ran round through the right.

Then we came to face daisies. These beasts could eat us without needing to poison us.

"Can't we use the meat trick again, since they too are carnivores?" Rian asked.

"No. We've run out of meat, and the daisies saw the meat trick! We'll have to find another way through," I said.

"Can't we just go back and look for another way?" Gian asked.

Just then, I saw Isabelle's charm

bracelet!

"We can't just go back, we're definitely on the right track. Look, Isabelle's charm bracelet!"

Rian and Gian gasped. " Oh, yes!" they said at the same time.

"Wait! I have an idea!" I made a stick out of water with my water powers, stuck it firmly on the ground, pulled it back, let it go and went flying over the daisies.

Then I signalled the others to do the same. Oh, and during my free but short flight over the daisies, **Isabelle's** bracelet got stuck on my pants. I just took a step when I heard something fall to the ground, it was the charm bracelet! But it was red. **Isabelle** was in danger.

There were tall bushes; we pushed them aside and found ourselves surrounded by more bushes. Uh-oh, I didn't have a good feeling about this. I just took a step when a huge and heavy metal cage fell over us. I had stepped on a button which triggered the cage to fall down. I had quickly dodged out of the way, and so did **Rian** and **Gian**.

Then we saw a glint of a man/woman charging towards us, like a bull! I jumped up into the air, showing off my split in the air, so I dodged him/her.

Rian and **Gian** cartwheeled out of the way, but the mysterious man/woman didn't give up. Why am I calling him/her mysterious? Because I just could not make out the face. He/she was wearing a dark hood and a mask over his/her face. Then he/she disappeared into the shadows.

A moment later, a blast of super-sticky slime hit **Rian**, and he was stuck to the tall bushes; the same thing happened to **Gian**. Uh-oh, I was the only one standing, and I had to face him/her alone. He/she tried to shoot it at me, but I was 1 step ahead of him/her. I used my acrobatic moves to dodge it. Then he/she took out a second one, but again I was 1 step ahead. You see, my wristbands have built-in slime shooters, which shoot extra, extra sticky slime, three on each hand. I touched both my wristbands, and they activated. I shot it at him/her and he/she was sticked onto a tree.

I came up, took off the hood and mask, and guess who it was, it was **Arabella!** The most slimiest sewer rat (she is not a rat and she does not live in the sewers) in all our adventures. But I have to admit it is fun. We capture her and let her stay captured. Then her family has to rescue her. They always try to get revenge, but we always outsmart them.

Now we just have to find **Isabelle**. Then we saw her. She was trapped in the petals of a lotus. Well, I was a brainiac in science, chemistry and physics. I made the antidote, duplicated it and gave some bottles to **Rian**, then freed **Isabelle** and gave some bottles to her. Once the garden was not a peculiar plant jungle, we immediately booked a flight back to Bahrain. So, you know what happened on the flight.

CATZILLA

Hi! My name is **SAVANNAH**, and I'm one of the **POWER SQUAD!** Why am I sooo calm? Because I'm just feeding my cat.

Ahhhhhh!!!!! Why am I screaming like a maniac? Ahhhhhh!!!!! My cat just turned into **'CATZILLA'** and is tearing the city down.

Ahhhhhh!!!!! **Arabella!!!** I know it's you, show yourself! Then out came **Arabella** holding the **"VILLAN CAT FOOD"**, she was fidgeting with it when she saw the monster coming to me!

I pointed my finger at her, and to my surprise, it took heavy steps toward her. She was still laughing like a maniac when the monster stepped on her and squashed her like a pancake. Taking advantage, I rolled her into a ball and kicked her to the moon! (well, not really to the moon, just far away) Well, at that time, **Rian**, **Isabelle** and **Gian** were there too. I told them to try and control **'CATZILLA'**. Then I ran back to my house.

What for? I ran to my house, opened my secret lab. And after many failures, I finally accidentally created: **IYCTICUT**. It sounds weird, but I chose this name because each letter is the initial of a word. I will tell you about it. If your cat turns into **'CATZILLA'**, use this. So, I went out, took an empty swimming pool and filled it with **IYCTICUT**.

Well, I have the ability to make noises really loud, and when I say really, I mean intensively, and when I say intensively, I mean... well, you get the point, right?

Anyway, I whistled and pointed at the food. Oh, and my cat's name is Lucy. Lucy saw me and started eating. As soon as she finished eating, she shrank back into my sweet Lucy's form! I'm so happy to have her back!

My fellow partners and I were sooo relieved that we didn't have to deal with **'CATZILLA'** anymore.

SCISSOR PLIGHT

H-ahhhhhh!!! Eeeeek!! Yow! Phew, I don't think they will find us here.

Oh, hi! I guess I don't need an introduction, well, I don't even have time! We are fighting something. I'll tell you how it began. So like us, **Arabella** is a child and is in our school! **Gunther**, her father, threatened to blow up our school if they refused to let her join the school. So we had to let her in. And I think they had a reason to put us in the same class.

But there is a disadvantage, everyone is a wimp in my class! But today's problem is that she wanted to go to the washroom, but the washroom is near the KG sections. And she made a potion to turn things into chaos. So she poured a drop onto each child's table and told, "Dip your scissors into the liquid!" and that's what happened. Wait! I totally forgot!

I'm still in my normal form! In fact, everyone was!

I whisper-shouted, "Everyone, take your super flower-eeeek!" I was interrupted by **Rian's** shrill scream.

The scissors found us! We were trapped. But don't worry, cause we were transformed and ready to fight. First, they tried to box our ears* but we boxed theirs back.

Next, they tried to kick us, but they barely did. Then they tried to cut our hair, but they could cut: 0 strands of our hair, 0 inches and 0cm. Then I remembered, we've got to find their weakness! Rocks! Of course!

Luckily, there were some huge ones. We threw them, and they got jammed. Then we got the strongest rope in the world, tied the scissor, carefully removed the rocks and really tied them up.

The next day, my team found me sleeping. On my bedside table was a test tube filled with a popping liquid. Sticked on it was a note saying "I'm sleeping as I stayed up all night making a potion. The liquid you see is the potion to minimize the scissors to their regular form. Pour 1 drop into each scissor. They sighed and did as told while I snored away.

A FORTY WINKS NIGHT

Yawn. Uhhhh. *Grrrrr* (me yawning and making grunting sounds) yawn.

"I'm so sleepy, but I can't sleep." I said.

"Me too." Rian said.

"Me three." Isabelle said.

"Me four." Gian said.

We all burst out laughing, and then went back to our sleepy mode. I looked out of my window and saw that every window's light in every building in our town was switched off!

When my friends came to check on me, they found me with a perplexed* face.

"What occurred?" They asked.

I was too aghast* to reply. Right at that moment someone all dressed in black smashed through our window. It was hard to see his face in the candlelight. *Wait, did I mention our house ran out of electricity? Whatever.* Then, without warning, a dazzling* light blinded us for a moment.

When we opened our eyes, a **blue-lit**

rope was coiled around us, and it was rigorous*to remove. Then the man sneered (at least I thought he did, maybe he did something else) at us. I felt something sharp pricking me.

It was a piece of glass! Our only hope to escape! Slowly and carefully, I was able to break the rope. Then we reached out for our superpens.

But... but... I don't want to tell you this, but okay. Our superpens are nowhere to be seen! Yup! Oh, dread. It must have been that mystery guy. *Grrrrrr* (me gnashing my teeth).

"I'll have to do this mission myself." I said.

"Why?" Asked the others.

Then they started begging to go with me. Finally, I couldn't take it anymore and I agreed.

"But", I said, "first let's discuss who it might be."

Then, after discussing it for a long time, we still have no clue who he was. Then I got an idea! I rapidly started typing on my computer, and finally found out who he was! I did it using my ethical hacking skills! (I'm an ethical hacker.) Then I hacked into his account and traced his location.

"It seems that his name is Mark, and that he is **Arabella's** elder brother!"

"Hip hip hooray!" The others chanted.

"Three cheers for Savannah!"

I blushed.

Then we went out the front door, and I locked it 3 times, and before that, I put 4 layers of laser-proof glass on the windows. Then, we were ready to go. I made sure everyone had their gear.

So, phone in hand, we followed the GPS to his house in Rottington. There the plan went exactly as planned. We had a sneak attack, and was able to capture them and hand them to the police!

OFF THE LIMITS

Café

Hi! I... guess I don't need to introduce myself, but here is the story... So it all began when the **POWER SQUAD** and I were playin' the Roblox game, adopt me, then we all felt a tingling sensation, then a burning sensation, then a fizzy sensation, and then in the blink of an eye, we were in... in... in the game!

So there we were in the game, looking totally confused. Then something caught our eye (not in a good way).

Can you guess what it was? An ocean of phirannas? A noob? Nope, none of them. it was... was... **Arabella** is in the game! Yes, **Arabella** right there, in front of our eyes, in the game...

"Ooh-la la" she said, "what a surprise!" Then she made a fake ringing sound, and then she said "oops gotta go, bye" and was out of the scene in a flash.

And if you're wonderin' how I made out that **Arabella** was makin' fake ringin' sounds, then trust me, BOYS and GIRLS, it's so easy to make out what sounds are real and what are fake when **Arabella** makes the sound.

Anyway, we decided we would just enjoy ourselves until **Arabella** came by.

Soon enough, disaster struck. We went to the café and then the café blasted. We were, luckily, not too badly hurt, but we were still hurt. In the hospital, the only name I muttered under my breath was **Arabella**.

The doctor said that the others were okay and were ready to be discharged, but I was still badly hurt and they needed to do surgery. I was shocked, but still managed to say "okay, I guess", then a spark of recognition came into my eyes.

"Doc, could you just take down your mask for a sec?" I politely asked. She hesitated, but she did it cause if she did not, then she would get fired.

And then I said OL (out loud), "Hello 'FAKE' doctor Arabella."

Then the rest of the **POWER SQUAD**

and the manager came rushing into our room and stared at us like we were mad.

Then the manager asked, "Excuse me doctor what is your name?"

Then she said, "Mary".

Then the manager said, "but the doctor assigned for the patient is phillip".

Then he said, "you're an imposter. You don't work here."

I quickly said, "She also said that I needed surgery. When I was completely okay! My friends also suffered from the same thing as me at the same time. Also, her name is not Mary, it's Arabella, she's our worst enemy."

Then Arabella said in a villainous voice, "Yep, I'm their worst enemy, and I'm the one who blasted the café, Savannah. How babyish of you to not see me following you."

"What?! You were following us?😠" I asked.

"How dare you, spoiled brat!" (you see I have a very short temper).

"Calm down!" The POWER SQUAD told

me in perfect unsion like they've practiced it a million times! But to be honest with you guys... we've never practiced!

Then, suddenly we heard a pop and we were back in our room.